Mind MATTER

TAREVA L. WATTS, LLMSW

ISBN: 9798730398719

MIND OVER MATTER

TABLE OF CONTENTS

THANKS&DEDICATION

Dear God, thank you. Simply thank you, for using me as a vessel to pour into the lives of others through this daily affirmation, with spiritual insight and perspective daily guide. Thank you, for seeing that I am equipped to walk through this 7-day journey with the reader of this guide. Thank you, God, for choosing me!

-Gratefully, your daughter

This book is dedicated to my family; My husband of thirteen years (he is my rock, my purpose, and biggest inspiration), my fifteen-year-old daughter, and my ten-year-old son, whom I love dearly with my whole heart soul, and soul. They have been my major support in all that I have put my mind to, and have achieved over the years. Thank you, and I love you.

Thank you, mama; you have implemented so many great qualities within me. I aspire to be more like you daily. You are a loving, powerful, bold, and supportive individual. Most of all, the love that you have towards God is indescribable, and I admire that about you! Thank you for showing me that with God on my side, I can achieve absolutely anything. Thank you for always believing in me mama. I love you.

Thank you to my mother-in-law; my "bonus mom", who has always supported me and my family over the years. Thank you for the ongoing love, support, and dedication that you have always expressed and demonstrated. I love you.

Thank you to my two sisters, Tempresse, and Madison, for always believing in me; and a special thanks to two incredibly special people that I consider to be remarkably close to; they are more than a friend to me; they are my bonus sisters, Thank you, Motif, and Crystal. Thank you for always being supportive of my dreams and being more than a friend to me. I love you ladies.

Thank you to all my family, including my extended family, for always loving and supporting me through all of my endeavors. Words cannot express how grateful that I am to have all of you as part of my life. I have one of the best support systems that anyone could ever have. Thank you and I love you!

ABOUT THE BOOK

The intent of this daily guide is to encourage you as your sister in Christ through the utilization of daily insight, affirmation, and scripture. This daily guide is for the individual who needs that extra support, and or motivation to make it through their work week, or personal life on a day-to-day basis. It may seem easier to give up on yourself, and to feel as though you can't make it. There are so many obstacles, hurdles, and challenges that you may face; some of which you did not anticipate. How does that make you feel? For most, it may make you feel that you can't make it, or that you were not made to overcome your daily challenges, and that you should just throw in the "towel". As believers in Christ, we know that we can always lean and depend on Jesus to make it from day-to-day. However, it does not mean that things are not challenging at times; and you are left with various emotions and feelings that make you want to just surrender and give up. It is okay to have these emotions, as it is "normal". Just know that our maker, and creator, Christ Jesus, is there and that He hears your silent tears. I hope that you find comfort in this daily, guide and receive the spiritual perspective that is embedded within it's pages. Take this insightful perspective and implement it into your daily routine; as it should help your mindset to shift positively.

AFFIRMATION= noun
1. The action or process of affirming something or being affirmed.
2. Emotional support or encouragement.

MESSAGE FROM THE AUTHOR

This daily guide was written with divine purpose and individual direction from the Lord. I always envisioned myself writing a book; but I thought that my first book was going to be a book all about my life, life's challenges, and how I overcame them. I am here to tell you that God's timing is perfect; and it is without mistake. I was given directive from the Lord to write this 7-day spiritual affirmation guide for both the struggling individual, and the one who is craving motivation and affirmation to make it through the week. I was told to walk through each day of the week from my outlook and encourage the reader through my own feelings and perspective. I said, "Okay Lord, okay Lord." He said, "No, like, now get up and write; start with Monday, and end on Sunday," So, I listened; because I have learned that Obedience is better than sacrifice. Before you knew it, I was up and out of bed at 6:57 a.m, and began writing. I encourage you to listen to the voice of the Lord, pay attention to all of the signs, and follow his lead; he will never lead you astray. Although I am a Limited Licensed Master Social Worker (LLMSW), and I am used to automatically providing oversight, perspective, encouragement and much more; this vision, and experience was different for me. My hopes are that you feel supported and encouraged, and that you can make it through this day most of all. See each day as a new day; a day that God has granted you to have as another chance and opportunity. You can make it.

Love, Your sister in Christ
-Tareva Watts, LLMSW

beginning of the week

MONDAY

"This is the day which the Lord has made; we will rejoice and be glad in it" (Psalms 118: 24 KJV)

MONDAY INSIGHT

"Monday blues!" Many do not look forward to this day of the week. You may feel an abundance of overwhelming emotions; which can cause you not to show gratitude for this day of the week. You may feel as if you must face all of the obstacles, challenges, and hurdles that this day may bring. It may even feel as though you have brought all of the issues from the past week into this day that we call "Monday;" leaving you to feel an abundance of emotions and stress. You may have even gone as far as saying things like; "I hate Monday's," or, "is it the end of the day yet?" Your cohort, peers, family, or friends may nod their heads in agreement while making negative gestures regarding this day, not making it any better for you. Yeah, this is what I call Monday blues. Although, many of you may experience these emotions; that can change today. Yes, I said it; that can change right now and today. Change your Mindset this Monday.

Approach this day knowing that you can and will conquer whatever this day has in store for you. This day is not your previous Monday, it is a Monday that you have never seen before. Go into this day prepared, with a renewed mindset that this is another day that God has granted you to see, feel, touch and experience. Yes, you got it; this is a day of a new chance and opportunity.

You have control of this day that we call Monday. This day will set the tone for the rest of your week. Take the three p's (patience, plan, prepare) with you on this day and make the best of your Monday.

1. Patience: Be patient with yourself, knowing that you are in control
2. Plan: Create & Plan your week
3. Prepare: Prepare yourself for the rest of this day, and week knowing that there may be ups and downs to it; you are in control

Daily
AFFIRMATION/SCRIPTURE

AFFIRMATION

No matter what today's challenges may bring; hold your head up high, put your shoulders back and know that you can overcome them. Be the change that you wish to see. Look at this day as one that you have never seen before and that you must conquer in order to get to the next day.

SCRIPTURE

"This is the day which the Lord has made; we will rejoice and be glad in it"
(Psalms 118: 24KJV.)

MINDSET MONDAY

SELF-CARE & MINDFULNESS STRATEGY

Breathing techniques: Inhale & Exhale slowly as many times as you can tolerate, "Know that you are breathing in your challenges and exhaling that you are in control."

JOURNAL YOUR EXPERIENCE:

_____

_____

_____

_____

_____

_____

_____

Monday's Twin

TUESDAY

"For we walk by faith, not by sight" (2 Corinthians 5:7 KJV)

TUESDAY INSIGHT

"Take-Over" Tuesday. You have conquered Monday and made it to Tuesday. Hello Tuesday! This is a day where you may be feeling a little more enthused and that you have a little more control. You may have 129 million-plus thoughts that may be going through your head at this point. On this day, you may feel as if you are moving in the right direction and that your thought and plans are clearer. You may even dive headfirst into some things, not knowing what the outcome may be; but you have faith and believe that your plan is going to work out. On the other hand, you may still feel the need to worry about the previous day and what you didn't accomplish; you know, Tuesday's twin; Monday. The reason you may be experiencing overwhelm, is that your mindset was not initially organized and shifted, leaving it in a disarray. I am here to tell you, that those thoughts do not have to exist any longer. You are taking control of this Tuesday. Why? Because with the direction of Christ and a refocused mindset; YOU ARE IN CONTROL.

Daily
AFFIRMATION/SCRIPTURE

AFFIRMATION

Drink your coffee and take complete control of this day. This is your chance to restore, and rejuvenate, and move forward. God has given you power over your circumstances.

SCRIPTURE

"For we walk by faith, not by sight." (2 Corinthians 5:7 KJV)

TAKE-OVER TUESDAY

SELFCARE & MINDFULNESS STRATEGY

·

*"Call a friend or a person that you
are close to and discuss your day. This helps to alleviate your daily stressors."*

JOURNAL YOUR EXPERIENCE:

·

_____

_____

_____

_____

_____

_____

_____

Centered and Grounded
WEDNESDAY

"I can do all things through Christ which strengthened me" (Philippians 4:13 KJV)

WEDNESDAY INSIGHT

Wednesday is a day where you may feel that you have got this! As you do!! This a day where you may have felt that you are becoming more centered and grounded. Many refer to this day as, "hump-day," meaning, that you have made it to the middle of the week, and are heading towards the end of the week it; yet so eager for the entire week to be over. Do not give up on yourself. Despite the tired feeling that you may be experiencing related to your workday; and the things you have to do at home, keep pushing. You are making great progress and improvement. Forget about the flaws and glitches; Wednesday has arrived, and you are persevering through this day. Take a second to realize that you have made this far, and it is okay to give yourself credit for your accomplishments. Although you may feel as if you struggled to get to this point, you did it, and you have included changes that have worked for you to get to this point. Keep going; you are on the right path. Change those things that didn't work and modify them as you see fit. It is ok. You are now centered, and ready to push through the rest of the week. You are not alone, don't give up!

Daily
AFFIRMATION/SCRIPTURE

AFFIRMATION

You have arrived! You have mastered half of your week. Look at all of the positives and give yourself a pat on the back; You deserve it. You are beating all of the odds that may have attempted to disrupt your week! Keep pushing, you have made it too far to stop now!

SCRIPTURE

"I can do all things through Christ which strengthened me" (Philippians 4:13

KJV)

WORTHY WEDNESDAY

SELFCARE & MINDFULNESS STRATEGY

"Take an hour to yourself, doing something that you find peace; and comfort in doing. This time should serve as space for you to process and allow your thoughts to roam freely."

JOURNAL YOUR EXPERIENCE:

_____

_____

_____

_____

_____

_____

_____

Accomplished vs. Not enough days in the week

THURSDAY

"O magnify the Lord with me, and let us exalt his name together"

(Psalms 34:3 KJV)

THURSDAY'S INSIGHT

Oh yes, it is Thursday! A day that is comforting to many of us. For most of you, this may feel as if you can see the light at the end of the tunnel. You may feel that you have made significant gains at this point in the week. However, there may be some of you that are feeling as though there are just are not "enough days" in this week; leaving you to feel as though you are starting from scratch. Please understand that it is okay to start over. It is okay to push the reset button. It is okay that you have not completed everything that you listed on your to-do list at this point. It is okay! Give yourself permission to be thankful, showing gratitude for all of your efforts both good and bad that you have put forth with the help from our Lord. Be thankful and take it easy on yourself. Take it one- task- at a time.

Daily
AFFIRMATION/SCRIPTURE

AFFIRMATION

It is okay to start over again. You are your own competition. Reset your mindset and be thankful for this Thursday. Continue to seek God through this day; he will see you through it. Rather than looking at the negatives of this day; look at the positives and give thanks to the Lord for seeing fit for you to endure today's challenges.

SCRIPTURE

"O magnify the Lord with me, and let us exalt his name together" (Psalms 34:3 KJV)

THANKFUL THURSDAY

SELF-CARE & MINDFULNESS STRATEGY

·

"Take fifteen minutes to jot down your thoughts that may be roaming through your head, allowing your space to be devoted to your internal feelings."

JOURNAL YOUR EXPERIENCE:

·

_____

_____

_____

_____

_____

_____

_____

I made it! Thank God the week is over

FRIDAY

"Let your light so shine before men, that they may see your good works, and glorify your Father which is in heaven" (Matthew 5:16, KJV)

FRIDAY INSIGHT

T.G.I.F! Yes, I know what you are thinking; everything has come to an end, and all that you have to do is make it through today. Your agenda may be a little lighter; and for some of you, it may be a little heavier. Anyhow, the positive is that today is Friday. You may be experiencing something called the "Friday Blues." This may feel as though all of your energy is depleted, and that you are left empty. Meaning, you may feel like you have absolutely nothing left to offer anyone at this point in the week, and all that you want is for this day to be completely over. Just when you think that you do not have anything else to offer, a situation arises that causes you to have to interject and fulfill whatever void at that moment. It's okay; you were chosen for this exact moment. The works that you have completed thus far, are the works from the Lord. Continue to follow the Lord's plan, and you will be replenished. Your hard work, dedication, loyalty, and efforts are noticed!

Daily
AFFIRMATION/SCRIPTURE

AFFIRMATION

Hey you; yes you... keep going! Others are relying upon you. You have divine purpose and destiny. Protect your space and fulfill it with positivity. Do not let anything or anyone dim your "light bulb."

SCRIPTURE

"Let your light so shine before men, that they may see your good works, and

glorify your Father which is in heaven." (Matthew 5:16, KJV)

TAKE-OVER FRIDAY

SELF-CARE & MINDFULNESS STRATEGY

Embrace yourself:
"Take a mental note, and tell yourself that you are enough! Let yourself know how impactful and needed that you are."

JOURNAL YOUR EXPERIENCE:

_____

_____

_____

_____

_____

_____

_____

Catch up day-overwhelmed-intense

SATURDAY

"In all thy ways acknowledge him, and he shall direct thy paths."
(Proverbs 3:6, KJV)

SATURDAY INSIGHT

This is a day where you may be playing catch-up. You may have created another to-do list to try and complete the task that you were not able to complete during the week. You may have an overwhelming list filled with lists; leaving you to have feel as if you just can't accomplish them all today. This feeling is absolutely normal to have. How about taking a step back, and re-evaluating everything that you have listed. Try a different approach to attacking your Saturday duties; complete one task at a time. If you have household duties to complete; complete one area or room of your home at a time. It will be there; please stop overwhelming yourself with today's tasks. It will get done!

Daily
AFFIRMATION/SCRIPTURE

AFFIRMATION

It is okay that you had a long list today; but, tell yourself that in order for you to take in this Saturday that you must be sane in doing so. Give yourself permission to modify your Saturday to what works best for you. This is your catch-up day; and you have control over how smoothly or rough it may go. Always allow the Lord to lead, direct, and guide you, and be the driver in all that you do. Trust me, it works out better this way. The Lord will never leave you!

SCRIPTURE

"In all thy ways acknowledge him, and he shall direct thy paths."

(Proverbs 3:6, KJV)

SELFCARE SATURDAY

SELF–CARE & MINDFULNESS STRATEGY

.

"Take time in the midst of your catching up to think of yourself after your long and intense week. Take everything into consideration, and process it all."

JOURNAL YOUR EXPERIENCE:

.

_____

_____

_____

_____

_____

_____

Day of rest the 'sabbath day'

SUNDAY

"For I know the plans I have for you, says the Lord. They are plans for good and not for disaster, to give you a future and a hope." (Jeremiah 29: 11, NLT)

SUNDAY INSIGHT

Sunday, Sunday, Sunday. This is a day where many may practice their religious and spiritual beliefs, which may include them going to church, or fellowshipping with family members and close friends. Many people have been taught to dedicate this day to the Lord, and not to do much of anything on this day, as it should be kept holy. Meaning, this is supposed to be a very calm and relaxing day in acknowledging the Lord. I know, I understand what you are thinking at this point in the week. This is a day where you are still cleaning, cooking, and planning out your endless calendars for the next week. Trust me, I get it. However, it is okay to say to yourself that you are going to take rest and relaxation, while implementing your spiritual beliefs and practices. This is a very important time to talk to the Lord, asking him to please lead and guide you through your upcoming week, allowing you to have productivity through your plans and purpose. He knows you best; and he knows what the next week will intel. A mindset is a powerful tool that you must take control of. Tell yourself how this day will look, and set boundaries allowing this day to be uninterrupted. Spend time with the Lord, yourself, and with your family.

Daily
AFFIRMATION/SCRIPTURE

AFFIRMATION

You are being led in the right direction. The Lord wants you to do well, and for you to prosper. Live this day knowing that God has chosen you, so do not think that you were not made for this. He will give you what you can handle, as he holds the ultimate plans.

SCRIPTURE

" For I know the plans I have for you, says the Lord. They are plans for good and not for disaster, to give you a future and a hope" (Jeremiah 29: 11, NLT)

REST & RELAXATION SUNDAY

SELFCARE & MINDFULNESS STRATEGY

*"This space should be filled with you resting, relaxing, and rejuvenating.
Remember that even Jesus took the time to rest."*

JOURNAL YOUR EXPERIENCE:

_____

_____

_____

_____

_____

_____

_____

CLOSING ENCOURAGEMENT

Dear Friend,

Thank you for taking the time to read this guide; and express your daily thoughts and emotions in your provided journal. It was designed just for you. I pray that this guide has touched you as it has touched me. My prayers are that you have received the motivation, connection, mindfulness techniques, and insight that you deserve. More importantly, my hopes are that you feel as though you have given this week all that you could, knowing that you are enough, and that your best is all that is required each day. Remember to approach each day with a positive mindset; your mind is a powerful tool and remembers that you have control over it. Make each day a great day by embracing each moment that it may bring. Whenever you feel that you have not accomplished all of your week's goals, look at the small things that you have accomplished and give yourself praise for it. This should bring you assurance, and a sense of satisfaction. Continue to allow God to direct your paths in all that you do, and you will always succeed.

Best blessings,

Tareva Watts, LLMSW

Made in the USA
Monee, IL
31 December 2022

20056951R00026